# So What About Soil?

## A Book About Form and Function

Rachel Chappell

Rourke
Publishing LLC
Vero Beach, Florida 32964

www.rourkepublishing.com

PHOTO CREDITS:  title page © Craig Barhorst;  P04 © Jennifer Nickert;  P05 © Anita Patterson Peppers;  P06 © Dhoxax;  P06a © Henry Hazboun;  P07 © Bruce Amos;  P08 © Kim Sarah Bernard;  P10 © Julie Felton;  P11 © Gordana Sermek;  P12 © Sierpniowka;  P14a © Andrey Grinyov;  P14b © Tootles;  P15a © Daemys;  P15b © Peter Jochems;  P15c © Bogdan Radenkovic;  P17 © Joe Gough;  P18 © Wendy Kaveney Photography;  P19 © Andrew F. Kazmierski;  P20 © Styve Reineck;  P21a © Thomas M. Perkins;  P21b © Mypokcik;  P22 © Heather A. Craig

Editor: Robert Stengard-Olliges

Cover design by Michelle Moore.

**Library of Congress Cataloging-in-Publication Data**

Chappell, Rachel M., 1978-
  So what about soil? : a book about form and function / Rachel Chappell.
      p. cm. --  (Big ideas for young scientists)
  Includes index.
  ISBN 978-1-60044-540-8 (Hardcover)
  ISBN 978-1-60044-701-3 (Softcover)
  1.  Soils--Juvenile literature.  I. Title.
  S591.3.C43 2008
  631.4--dc22
                                          2007018565

Printed in the USA

CG/CG

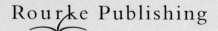

Rourke Publishing

www.rourkepublishing.com – rourke@rourkepublishing.com
Post Office Box 3328, Vero Beach, FL 32964

# Table of Contents

# The Importance of Soil

Bits of rock, living organisms, and plant and animal pieces crunch beneath our feet every day. Have you ever stopped to think about how important the **soil** below us really is?

Without soil there would be no plants, and
without plants there would be no people. Soil
is the source of water and **nutrients** for plants.
And, soil holds the roots that support plants.

**Cactus**

The amount of water, nutrients, and air in soil are **attributes** that affect which plants grow in the soil. Plants grow best where the soil's attributes meet their needs.

# Calla Lilly

For example, a cactus needs little water, therefore it grows well in a desert soil that holds little water. Calla lilies need a lot of water to thrive, so they grow best near the water's edge where the soil stays very moist.

# Soil Components

**Components of soil**

- minerals
- air
- water
- plant and animal products

Soil is made of several parts, or **components**. The components give soil its form. Small, broken pieces of rock are one component.

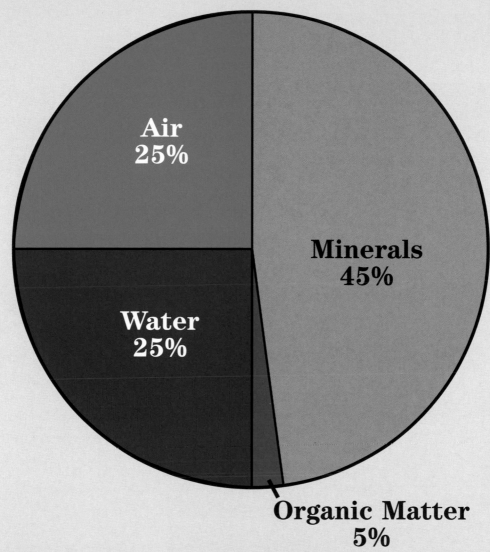

*This pie chart shows the average components of soil.*

Living organisms like fungi and bacteria are also part of soil. They break down, or decay, organic matter including such things as dead leaves, grass, and wood.

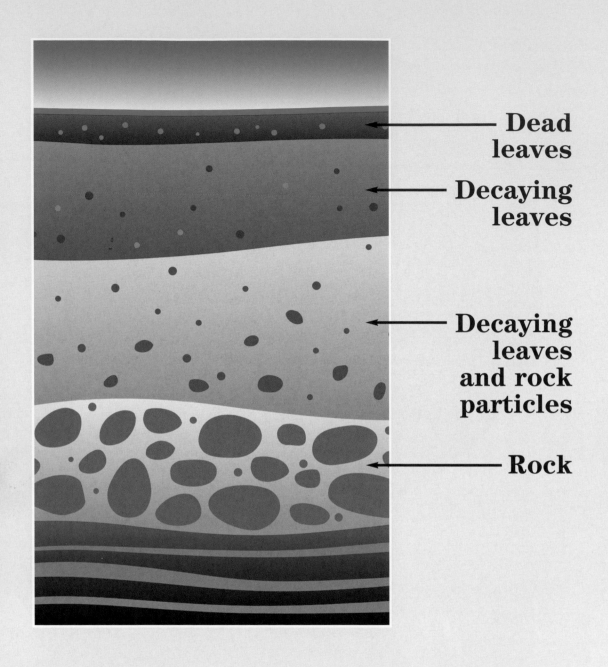

**Dead leaves**

**Decaying leaves**

**Decaying leaves and rock particles**

**Rock**

Small pieces of plant material are found in soil. Small animals such as mice and moles take seeds and other plant parts into underground burrows where the plant parts decay and become part of the soil.

10

*Worms help make soil richer.*

Earthworms digest organic material, recycle the nutrients, and make the soil richer. Animal matter from their poop and the decay of their dead bodies, become part of the soil.

Besides light, most plants need food
(nutrients), water, and air to survive. They
get some nutrients and water from the soil.
Nutrients dissolve in the water. They are
taken up by the plant's roots and used or
stored in the stems and leaves.

# Soil Attributes

## Deciduous forest regions
Soil is deep, rich, and dark brown in color

## Sandy region
Soil is dry and dusty gray in color

## Tropical regions
Soil is deep and bright red

Soil has different **textures**, colors, and water holding abilities. The type of soil found where you live, and its function, depends on the **climate**, the kind of rocks beneath the soil, and the plants that grow in the soil.

*Changing the texture can provide just the right growing conditions for plants.*

Soil texture depends on the size of its mineral **particles**. Particle size has a lot to do with how well the soil allows water to drain and the amount of nutrients it holds. These two factors determine what kind of plants can grow best in each soil.

Sand, silt, and clay are three main kinds of soil. Sand has the largest particles. Clay has the smallest particles, and silt particles are in the middle. Most plants grow best in combination soil.

*Consider this: If you compare the size of soil particles to something you know, sand particles would be the size of a medium sized watermelon. Silt particles would be the size of an apple, and each clay particle would be the size of a strawberry.*

**Sand Particle**

**Silt Particle**

**Clay Particle**

# Sand

Sand grains are the largest particles in the soil. Sand is rough, has sharp edges, and does not hold many nutrients for plants. Because the particles are bigger and they do not stick together, sand dries out quickly. This is a good thing for plants because their roots need oxygen. When standing water keeps a plant's roots from getting needed oxygen, the plant drowns.

*Fertilizer can be added to sand to increase levels of nutrients.*

Sandy soil is best for growing grass on golf greens and in football arenas. The sand doesn't compact and it drains well after a rain. Crops such as peanuts and strawberries grow well in light and sandy soil that warms quickly.

17

# Clay

*When clay dries out it is often hard like cement.*

Clay particles are very small. Clay soil is smooth when dry, but like sticky putty when wet. Clay holds lots of nutrients and water, but because it is so thick it doesn't hold much air. Clay soil can be difficult for plant growers to **cultivate**, or work with, when it gets wet.

Clay's ability to hold water well makes it valuable in a dry climate for plants that need a lot of water. Plum trees thrive in a stiff clay soil. They are hardy trees that require little attention but lots of water.

# Silt

*The Nile River in Egypt floods and then leaves behind rich silt. This fertile soil is good for growing many crops.*

Silt particles are larger than clay, but smaller than sand. Silt soil is not sticky when wet, but feels smooth. Most plants will grow best in a combination soil where nutrients, air, and water are all available.

In science we can observe stuff like soil. We look at soil's form and soil's function. By looking at soil's ability to hold water, air, and nutrients, we can determine what plants it will support best.

At one time you may have thought to yourself, 'So what about soil?' Now you know.

# Glossary

**attributes** (AT ruh byoots) — traits, qualities, or characteristics of a person, place or thing

**climate** (KLYE mit) — the general weather conditions of a region

**cultivate** (KUHL tuh veyt) — to prepare and work on land in order to raise crops

**decay** (da KAY) — to become decomposed; rot

**nutrients** (NOO tre uhnts) — a source of nourishment

**organic** (or GAN ik) — material from living plants or animals

**soil** (sOYL) — dirt where plants grow

**weathering** (WETH er ing) — processes that cause rock to decompose

# Index

## Further Reading

Cooper, Sharon. *Using Soil*. Heinemann Library, 2007.

Walker, Sally M. *Soil (Early Bird Earth Science)*. Lerner Publications Company, 2006.

Tomecek, Steve. *Dirt*. National Geographic, 2007.

## Websites to Visit

www.urbanext.uiuc.edu/gpe

school.discovery.com/schooladventures/soil

www.nrcs.usda.gov/feature/education/squirm/skworm.html

## About the Author

Rachel M. Chappell graduated from the University of South Florida. She enjoys teaching boys and girls as well as their teachers. She lives in Sarasota, Florida and gets excited about reading and writing in her spare time. Her family consists of a husband, one son, and a dog named Sadie.